MEDIA GOTHIC

A STROLL DOWN THE DARK HISTORY OF STATE STREET

A COMPANION BOOK
TO THE
MEDIA GOTHIC WALKING TOUR

BY LAURIE HULL AND MATT LAKE

FEATURING VINTAGE PHOTOGRAPHY FROM THE MEDIA HISTORIC ARCHIVES

STANDARD PAPERBACK EDITION   978-1-954895-00-3
HARDBACK EDITION   978-1-954895-01-0
BARGAIN PAPERBACK EDITION   978-1-954895-02-7

Published by
Media Gothic
P.O. Box 1461
Media, PA 19063

MediaGothic.com

MEDIA GOTHIC

IS MEDIA GOTHIC?

When we first began taking groups around the county seat of Delaware County, Pennsylvania, we decided to call our outings the Media Gothic Walking Tour.

One of the first questions we had to answer was "Is Media really Gothic?" It is, after all, Everybody's Home Town, and the first Fair Trade town in the United States. Back in the 1950s, they used to call Media "The Number One Town on the Number One Highway." (They were a bit long-winded in those days, but they clearly loved their town.)

All this makes Media sound lovely, wholesome, and pleasant—and it certainly is that, but we think it's pretty Gothic too. To understand what we mean by that, we have to explain what we mean by Gothic.

Are we suggesting Media is like goth music fans—pale, gloomy, dressed in black, and wearing dark eyeliner? Not so much. Is Media like Gothic architecture—sturdy, no-nonsense, and built to last? That's a little closer to the mark. Is Media like Gothic literature— dark, fantastical, full of madness, riddled with supernatural ghostliness, and rife with undertones of violence and death? Well, on occasions, yes it is. And that's why we named our tour—and this book—Media Gothic.

What you'll find in this book is a collection of historical accounts, true crime stories, and paranormal happenings from the Borough of Media. Each story here is tied to a place you probably walk past all the time. You may have shopped or gone to school at or eaten in a place with a strange history you never knew. You will know it now. Each of these stories is the result of in-depth research and interviews. We pored through books, archives, newspapers, and libraries. We spoke to dozens of people to get a balanced account. And thanks to the good people of the Media Historic Archives, we also unearthed some fantastic old photographs to illustrate them.

In the pages that follow, you will learn about some of Media's most notorious burglaries, murders, executions, crimes both large and small, plus madness, guns, ghosts, and one really large explosion.

Buckle up and brace yourselves: Media's dark history is a wild ride.

Laurie Hull and Matt Lake, Media, 2020

DETAIL FROM AN 1848 MAP OF DELAWARE COUNTY

SECTION I
BEFORE IT WAS MEDIA

BEFORE IT WAS MEDIA...

Before there was a State Street, before there was a trolley or courthouse, before there was a theatre and a big stone schoolhouse, the area we now know as the Borough of Media, Pennsylvania, was just farms, mills, and a blacksmith. The Borough's square mile back then was just a wedge of land hemmed in on both sides by two boundaries—one natural and one man-made.

To the west, there was a stream that powered mills that sheared lumber and ground up grain. We now call that stream Broomall's Run and the land around it has become Glen Providence Park, but at the time, it was called Scroggie Valley.

To the east was a main road that led from Chester to the northern towns of Delaware County—the Providence Great Road, now just called Providence Road. In fact, the area wasn't even called Media back then: it went by the name of Providence. It had no town center or stores, and the closest place of business was the Providence Inn at the corner of Providence Road and Baltimore Pike.

But before we launch in on tales of Media, let's first look at two tales that go back long before this place became the legal center of Delaware county. Let's go back to the days of Scroggie Valley, where the few scattered inhabitants untouched by the sophistication of busy towns saw evidence of supernatural activity everywhere—especially in their own back yards.

THE GHOSTS OF LOVE

The wooded valley that runs through what we now call Glen Providence Park is the home of two ghosts—or at least, two stories of ghosts that date back to before the War of Independence. We know about them because more than a century later, one of this area's most dedicated local historians, a retired doctor named Anna Broomall, retold their story in an article in the Chester Times in 1931.

The first apparition was a woman, who could be seen ranging along the valley from what is now the water treatment plant behind the Sterling Pig clear up to Broomall's Lake. At the time, her stamping ground started at a lumber mill near Baltimore Pike and continued along the bank of a fast-moving stretch of the river called a race bank. She could be seen going up and down the bank as if looking for something or someone.

Some time after she first appeared (in the late 1700s), people stumbled across a badly decomposed body in the nearby Iron Spring, nestled in the valley between Kirk Lane and present-day Media. The remains could not be identified, but one thing was certain—it was not the body that belonged to the roaming spirit.

These remains were of a man.

When the spirit of a man began to appear along the opposite side of the river, a full origin story took shape. These two were husband and wife, and the bride had died on their wedding day. This story sounds tragic—and of course, it is—but the details make it a lot less sentimental than it sounds at first.

The couple rode together on the same horse from the Rose Tree tavern (located on Providence Road opposite Kirk Lane) all the way to the Middletown Presbyterian Church to be married. It was a long ride there and back, and they made the trip alone, so nobody knew exactly what happened, but only the husband returned. The bride was never seen again—at least, in her bodily form.

Did they argue? Did she fall off the horse? Was she pushed? Was it all a tragic accident, or a crime of passion, or was it premeditated murder? Nobody can say for sure, but all these stories circulated. One thing was for sure: she died before her time, and her body was never found. Shortly afterwards, her spirit began to roam along a stretch of the river, perhaps trying to draw attention to her final resting place.

After the man's body was discovered, the locals made the connection that he had returned to the death scene in a fit of remorse, and overcome by the grief he felt at his lost love, or plagued by guilt at his part in her death, he took his own life. His suicide consigned his spirit to roam the earth, and because of what he did on his bride's last day on earth, he was condemned never to reunite with her, even in death.

THE WITCHES RIDE

At the corner of what is now Ridley Creek Road and Kirk Lane, there was once a stone building called Scroggie's Mill. A little upstream, near the location of Media's first waterworks and the current Aqua plant were several other small mills, some of which were rented out to tenants, but the area was mostly unsettled and far enough from any town that when the sun went down, it became dark and mysterious. It was just the kind of place where strange gothic stories of the supernatural could take hold—and sure enough, they did.

A strange circular pattern appeared on the hill directly to the west of what is now Front Street. It was about a hundred yards across, and it looked like a trail worn into the ground by hundreds of feet over dozens of months—except that it led nowhere and seemed to have appeared overnight. The locals immediately fell back on an old-country supernatural explanation—the pattern was caused by witchcraft somehow, and it was called a Witches' Ride.

Witches, they believed, would place people under a spell and force them to run around all night, leaving a trail that had not existed the day before. All the farmers, millers, and tenants in the area feared that this threat had followed them to the New World, and was manifesting itself on the hillside of Scroggie Valley.

As people retold the story in the early years of the 1800s, it soon incorporated a local character named Seth Levis as the hero who thwarted the witches. The version of the story that has lasted through the ages probably started as a party piece told by Seth Levis himself, because he certainly comes across as unusually wily and resourceful.

Seth Levis was a miller from a prominent local family who inherited a shingle mill from his father in 1798, and worked it until 1825. When the circular trail first appeared upstream from his mill, he knew what had caused it: Three old women, sisters, were renting a mill from Frank Cannon a ways upstream, and everybody knows witches come in threes and live by themselves in the woods.

To practice their enchantments, Seth would tell everyone, witches skulk around at night carrying an enchanted horse's bridle until they come to the home of a man who lives by himself. Making sure he is asleep, they sneak into his bedroom. If the door is locked, they can use an enchantment to slide in through the keyhole. Once inside, they glide quietly up to the bed, and before the man can wake, they throw the bridle across his face. By magic, the bridle transforms the man into a stallion, which the witch mounts and rides out of the house and up to a hilltop, where she drives it all night at a gallop. As the sun begins to rise, the witch removes the bridle to transform the horse back into a man. This happens more often that you would think, and it's why people often wake up feeling more tired than when they went to bed.

Seth Levis was determined not to be ridden all night by a witch, so when he heard a noise at his chamber door one night, he woke up ready to act fast. Sure enough, a witch entered and approached his bed as Seth lay quietly without moving, breathing regularly as if he were asleep. Before the witch could throw the bridle over his head, Seth snatched it from her and threw it over her head.

Since the magic was in the bridle, not in the witch herself, this bold move transformed the woman into a mare, and

Seth mounted her and rode her all night long. And just to be sure she would not escape and exact her retribution, he did not remove the bridle at dawn, but instead bolted her in the stable. Later that day, he took her to the blacksmith and had her hooves shod ready for another ride. And sure enough, he repeated the process at sundown too.

Exhausted from two long nights of riding, Seth decided that enough was enough and he released the mare from her bridle as the sun rose. She transformed back into human form and they both staggered back to their respective houses to rest.

Seth was sure to tell everyone about his exploits, and many people shrugged it off as a fiction.

However, not long afterwards, a rumor circulated that made people think that old Seth was telling the truth. One of the renters from Frank Cannon's house had visited the doctor. She asked to be treated for wounds on her hands and feet. The injuries looked almost as if she had been burned by horseshoes and scarred by nails.

THE CHARTER HOUSE

Site of a Cornfield where the first sale of Building Lots in Media was held September 17, 1849. The Charter House Association erected a Temperance Hotel in 1851 and it became a famous summer resort. Local elections were held here and Media Borough Council selected the hotel as its first permanent meeting site in August 1851. The original building remains in use as An Apartment House.

MEDIA BOROUGH COUNCIL, 1979

THE ORIGIN OF MEDIA

AND THEN, MEDIA HAPPENED...

Old rural folk tales like these began to fade away in the middle of the 1800s, when the modern commercial and government hub that we call Media sprang to life. But just because a sophisticated new town appeared where farms used to be, don't think that the strange stories of premature death and the supernatural dried up completely. They didn't.

So how did Media appear out of a rural farm-and-mill landscape full of ghost lore and witch tales? Well, it was a long time coming. For about thirty years, the good people of Delaware County were fed up with going all the way to Chester to conduct legal business. Things came to a head when the jailhouse and courthouse in Chester needed expensive repair, and the people of Delco finally stamped their feet and said "No! We won't pay!"

So another plan came about. A committee scouted out a suitably central location for a new courthouse and jail, and another figured out how to raise funds for it. They decided to buy up farmland in Providence and resell it as prime real estate to developers. They would use the profits to finance the new court and jail buildings. And that's how Media became the county seat of Delaware County.

And that's when the Gothic vibe really entered the area. Because no matter how much civilization tries to keep things orderly, Media has managed to keep its share of strange tales.

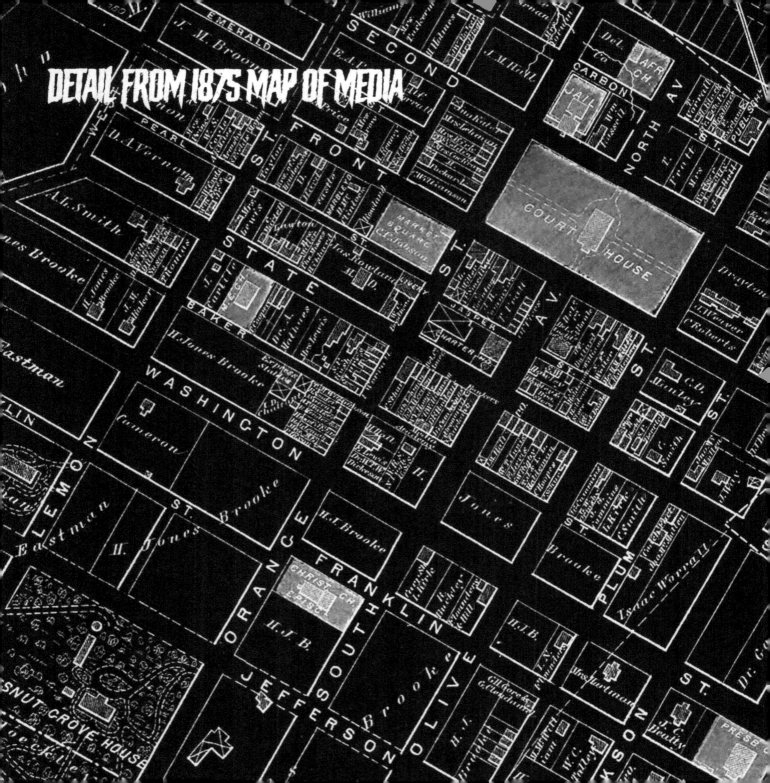

DETAIL FROM 1875 MAP OF MEDIA

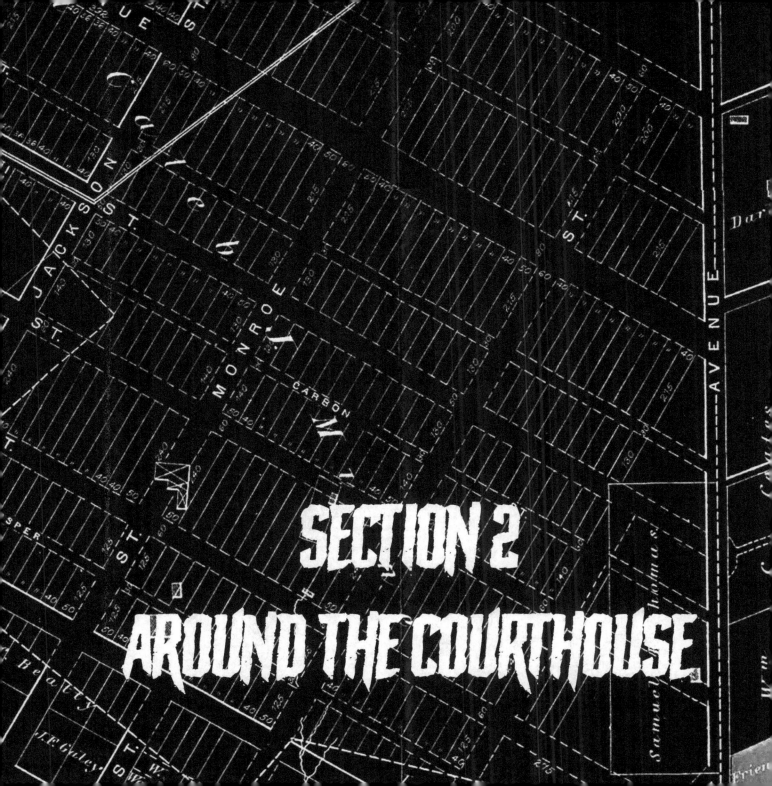

SECTION 2
AROUND THE COURTHOUSE

AN ORDINANCE

TO PREVENT

CORNER LOUNGING

AND

FAST DRIVING

IN THE

BOROUGH OF MEDIA.

Be it ordained and enacted by the Burgess and Town Council of the borough of Media, in Town Council assembled, and it is hereby enacted by authority of the same.

Sec. 1. That from and after the passage of this Ordinance, no persons shall assemble and lounge on any of the corners of any of the streets within said Borough, or create an annoyance to any of the inhabitants of said Borough, by assembling in front of any public or private property, or to obstruct the free passage of any sidewalk or highway of said Borough in any manner whatever.

Sec. 2. NO PERSON OR PERSONS SHALL RIDE OR DRIVE FASTER THAN AT THE RATE OF SIX MILES PER HOUR ALONG ANY STREET OR STREETS OF SAID BOROUGH.

Passed this Eleventh day of January, A. D., 1876.

C. R. WILLIAMSON,
President of Council.

Attest—A. P. OTTEY, Clerk.

Approved January 12th, 1876,

H. C. SNOWDEN, Chief Burgess.

Vernon & Cooper, Printers, Media, Pa.

THE BIRTH OF MEDIA

Media was designed from the ground up to be a place where people would want to live, work, and do business. There were even plans to make the Borough into a nice summer getaway for the people of Philadelphia. In short, everyone wanted Media to be the exact opposite of the old county town—and that meant they wanted no rowdy drunks or criminals causing trouble. So a group of well-meaning citizens pushed through a ordinance for the new borough: Media was going to be a temperance town. No liquor was to be bought, sold, or consumed there. And so for its first 80 years, you couldn't find intoxicating beverages anywhere in the Borough's square mile.

Other strict ordinances followed. Loitering was on street corners could land you in jail for 24 hours. Speeding through town was criminalized too—and the limit was set so low, you could probably be ticketed for running: It was illegal to go more than six miles an hour.

This did indeed make Media a desirable place to live, work, and visit. It was a nice, safe place. Whenever the Philadelphia Inquirer ran a story from the Borough, it would usually call it "the quiet temperance town of Media."

But even in a quiet temperance town, things can get dangerous or deadly or just plain weird. And in Media, they sometimes did. And the strangeness started where the town itself started—in the stretch of road we now call Veteran's Square leading up to the Courthouse.

CHARTER HOUSE

D. R. Hawkins, Proprietor

THE CHARTER HOUSE FROM STATE STREET 1855

THE CHARTER HOUSE

It's hard to imagine it now, but the apartment building we now know as Plymouth Hall at 20 Veteran's Square marks the spot where Media was born. In 1849, the land all around was just a cornfield marked out with stakes and this was the spot where people gathered to bid on plots that would become the Borough of Media. A big plot of land nearby was already allocated for the courthouse and jail, the rest was up for grabs. And a group of religious people organized by a pastor put in a bid for the plot of land where Plymouth Hall stands, hoping to build an attraction that would draw people from all around to Media. Their plan came to fruition and they built the building you see now, but they called it The Charter House, and it would be Media's premiere hotel...a hotel with a twist—you couldn't drink alcohol in it. It served as a public meeting place for the newly formed Borough Council until the first Borough Hall was built, and its rooms were filled to capacity by city folk looking for a getaway filled with good clean fun.

The Charter House's address was actually on State Street—it featured a huge suburban-style front yard with attractive trees and a lovely front porch to see it from. (You can't see it now because they built a bank in front of it, and now make you go through a side door to get into the building.)

After fifty years or so, the appeal of a temperance hotel had waned a little, and the Charter Hotel (as it was then named) had to hustle to get customers. One of the more peculiar advertising campaigns they dreamed up was to parade an elephant up State Street draped in a sheet with the words Charter Hotel painted on it. It's hard to say how effective that advertising was at the time, but in the long term, the hotel closed its doors and was converted into apartments under a new name.

Many hotels have ghost stories, but the Plymouth Hall apartments appear to be free of spirits—as you'd expect from a former temperance hotel. However, it does have one quirky story attached to it: During the 1984 election season, then-President Ronald Reagan visited Media to campaign for re-election. On the day before Halloween, he delivered a speech from the courthouse steps to a massive crowed that packed Veteran's Square all the way down to State Street. In the run-up to the visit, the Secret Service swept through all the buildings in range of the courthouse as a routine precaution to ensure the president's safety.

Two of the early walkers on the Media Gothic tour lived in a Plymouth Hall apartment at the time, and they told us this anecdote about the Presidential visit. Back then they were a young couple in their twenties, and most of the other residents were much older. Because the Secret Service doesn't announce security sweeps, they didn't know why there was a commotion in the hallway. So they cracked open their door and saw men in black suits carrying out armfuls of guns. They were baffled and a little scared, but found out that many of the residents had legal registered weapons in their possession, and the Secret Service impounded them until the visit was over.

Media already had a National Guard armory (it was on State Street in the building now occupied by Trader Joe's), but from the sheer number of guns taken out of Plymouth Hall that day, it looked like there was a pretty decent arsenal on Veteran's Square too.

THE JAILHOUSE

Media's jailhouse is no longer standing. It used to be next to the courthouse, set back a little on the northeast corner of Orange Street and Second Street. It was torn down in the 1950s, when it was barely 100 years old, as part of a courthouse expansion plan. The site of the old jailhouse is across the road from a field of gravel behind chain-link fence, and things weren't any cheerier when it was a jail.

When the courts and the jail moved to Media, all the inmates from the old jail in Chester came with them. There, they moved into new cells in a new building with a high wall and an exercise yard—and as a grim reminder of what could happen to hardened criminals, a gallows.

One of the main reasons for building a new prison was because the old one in Chester was falling apart and easy for prisoners to escape from. You would think this brand-new prison would be secure, but it only took three months for the first prisoner to scale the walls of the Media jail and escape. From that point on, escapes were rampant, and they had to remodel the prison several times to make it more secure.

But even though some people managed to cut their sentences short by running away, others never left the place at all—at least, not alive. In this section, we'll be looking at a couple of people who were serving short sentences but had the misfortune never to leave the building alive, and then we'll be looking at the three people who were executed there.

DEATHS IN THE JAILHOUSE

On February 7, 1879, Joseph Williams had come to the end of his sentence for assault and battery with a razor. He had been sentenced to one year but was given one month off his sentence for good behavior. He was not destined to enjoy his freedom.

On the morning of his release, Williams was overcome with stomach pains. He requested some ginger, but they ignored the request and told him to get ready to go. Shortly thereafter, he fell into convulsions and quickly died. The rapid onset of the illness, together with the extreme symptoms, gave rise to rumors that he had been poisoned. There was an inquest and despite the severity of the symptoms and the fact that the autopsy showed that the entire lining of his stomach was gone, the determination was death of natural causes. Did he know something he should not have? Was it revenge for some wrong he had done someone or was he just incredibly unlucky? Either way, he never made it out of Delaware County Prison alive.

He was not the only prisoner to die in unusual circumstances. On March 17, 1880, Richard Neeld was killed through another inmate's escape attempt. The man in the cell just above Neeld's, Martin O'Harra, had quite a plan to escape the newly fortified prison. He dug a hole in the chimneystack, through which he hoped to reach the roof. Digging produces debris, and his method of hiding the evidence was to throw it all down the chimneystack. Out of sight, out of mind. But the blocked flue prevented noxious fumes from fires from leaving the lower cells.

There were indicators that something was amiss: On March 15th, a prisoner in the lower cells fainted, but was revived. Then around dinnertime on the 17th, two other prisoners in lower cells were discovered to be insensible—but they also recovered. When they checked the next cell over, they found Richard Neeld, already dead. At this point the guards began searching for a cause and brought Martin O'Harra's escape plan to light. O'Harra then faced new charges and an increased sentence.

An investigation determined that the jail still provided too many opportunities to escape—but they didn't work out for the men on the next few pages.

ALBERT WEST IN HIS CELL – 1903

8252

1903
THE YEAR OF THE EXECUTIONS

Pennsylvania started carrying out executions in the 1600s by public hangings. They would take place in market squares or other places where the public could gather for a grim show. Killing criminals remained as a dark entertainment for the masses for another two hundred years, but this type of punishment didn't sit well with the Friends Meetings in the Quaker State. So in 1834, Pennsylvania became the first state to end public executions and move the gallows behind the walls of county prisons, where only invited witnesses could watch. Delaware County saw its fair share of executions in the old county prison in Chester, so when they finished building the county prison in Media in 1851, they made sure to include a gallows in the yard.

For 62 years, the gallows stood unused, serving only as a grim reminder of what could happen to people who committed premeditated murder, burglary, highway robbery, and even counterfeiting money. But in 1903, the political winds changed direction, and the County decided to make a tough stand against crime. And the convicts they singled out as examples were three men, all convicted of murder in the first degree.

ALBERT WEST

The first man to be executed by the county in the Media courthouse was Albert West. He was a hard man to defend: He was from out of town, so he had no family around to act on his behalf. He lived in a bad part of town. He was a heavy drinker. And the crime he had been convicted of was killing a police officer. Even so, there was a public outcry against executing him, but those voices were drowned out by demands for harsh penalties.

The day of the murder, Albert had been drinking heavily. His girlfriend, Addie Ballard was out in the city and he decided to try and find her, as he suspected she was keeping bad company. She had a habit of frequenting an area known as "Tinderbox Row", which was a rough area known for gambling dens and prostitution.

As he walked towards The Row, he stopped in a hardware store and bought a revolver. When he came out into the street, he met a friend who confirmed that Addie was indeed in Tinderbox Row. He ended up locating her there at a house where he had found her on former occasions. He was angry, and they began arguing. She agreed to go home with him, and they argued as they walked down the street, with West brandishing the gun and threatening to shoot Ballard. When they reached the intersection of Third and Pusey Streets, their disagreement attracted the attention of a police officer, Mark Allen.

Officer Allen had attempted to intervene and tried to take Albert West into custody when West fired the gun at the officer, hitting his leg and breaking it. The officer fell to the ground and West paused, then stepped back and shot him twice more, once in the head, which killed him. West fled the scene but was captured.

During the trial, West claimed that he was not responsible for his actions due to intoxication. This defense did not work, and he was found guilty of first-degree murder, which was upheld on appeal.

When he was handed a death sentence, there was a huge clamor for tickets to his execution. It was going to be the first execution in Media, and that made it a must-see event. It was also to take place on April 14th, which meant the weather would be nice.

But not everyone was so thirsty for blood. Quaker Meetings had lobbied for more lenient punishment than hanging, and local Quakers were so appalled at the sentence, they vacated town in protest on the day of the execution.

West's execution was so notorious that some people kept unusual souvenirs. You can see one of them, courtesy of Media Historic Archives Commission, in a display case upstairs at the Media-Upper Providence Public Library: It is the spoon West used in prison, with a black bow tied around it.

At the time of Albert West's execution, very few people left their bodies to medical science, but the cadavers of executed criminals were considered fair game to be cut up for practice by medical students. West was terrified this might happen to him, so left his body to the Catholic Church and asked that his grave be properly protected. This fear of being dissected would recur through Media's dark history, so be prepared to read about this more later.

ROBERT KILPATRICK

In August of 1903, a second man was hanged in the Media jail yard. His name was Robert Kilpatrick and he, too, had been found guilty of first-degree murder. In late 1901, Mrs. Bearmore began living with Robert Kilpatrick as his "housekeeper". Later her children testified that they had thought they were married.

In February of 1902, Mrs. Bearmore left the house to stay with her daughter because Kilpatrick was drunk and unruly. She stayed the night at her daughter's home and Kilpatrick sent a carriage to pick her up the next day.

Unfortunately, Kilpatrick was still drunk, or drunk again, when she returned home so she left and went back to her daughter's house. Robert Kilpatrick became angry and shortly after, followed her there with a gun in his pocket. When he arrived at the house, he said he was there for business and declared he would have her dead or alive. He began shooting and Mrs. Bearmore's son, Titus, tried to stop him. There was a struggle for the gun, and it is there that things become hazy.

Titus claimed that Robert wrested the gun away and aimed and shot at Mrs. Bearmore, hitting her in the chest and killing her instantly. Robert claimed that in the struggle for the gun, Titus fired it and that's how Mrs. Bearmore met her end. The only witnesses were Mrs. Bearmore's three children, who swore Kilpatrick had fired the killing shot in a moment of insanely jealousy, because he suspected she loved another man.

During the trial, Kilpatrick stuck to his story and feigned insanity. They even had witnesses testify that Kilpatrick often behaved strangely and erratically. This defense did not work, and he was found guilty of first-degree murder and sentenced to hang.

ROBERT KILPATRICK – BEFORE AND AFTER HIS TRIAL

Until the end, Kilpatrick swore that Titus and not he had fired the fatal shot.

On the date of his execution, the jail was under lockdown due to a smallpox epidemic. But even under such deadly conditions, 80 people were given tickets to attend the execution.

You can never underestimate the appeal of an execution: Even the people of the quiet temperance town of Media risked catching a painful and often fatal disease to see Robert Kilpatrick hang.

HENRY JONES

The last man executed in Media was Henry "Kid" Jones, who stood on the gallows shortly before Christmas 1903. His occupation is listed as gambler. His crime: First-degree murder of his wife. In a story like that of Albert West, who had been executed eight months before, Jones was intoxicated and went out looking to find his wife. He found her at the home of a woman he did not approve of. When he confronted her, she refused to leave with him, and he shot her.

After he was apprehended, he claimed to have no memory of the event because of his extreme state of intoxication. As in the previous two cases, this defense was not a good one, and he was sentenced to death. In an unusual twist, his defense team did not mount an appeal, even though public opinion was swinging away from enforcing the death sentence. As Christmas approached, demand for tickets proved to be even greater than it had been in the spring for the execution of Albert West. People believed, and rightly so, that this would be the last execution in Media.

Jones, like West, had a deep fear of his body being dissected after death, so he followed West's lead and left his body in the care of the Catholic Church. He knew that West had done this and received a proper burial.

Strangely enough, another murderer who had been buried in Delaware County seven years earlier had a similar fear and a similar insurance policy against being dug up and examined. Even more strangely than that, the Media Courthouse would have a hand in overthrowing the dead man's wishes.

To learn all about that, turn a few pages ahead to read about the strangest request ever to pass through the Delaware County Orphan's Court.

HENRY 'THE KID' JONES – BEFORE HIS EXECUTION

Court House & Jail.

TALES FROM THE COURTHOUSE

The Media Courthouse was intended to be the focal point of the whole town, so it took a while to build. Media was voted into existence in March 1850, and the final slap of wet plaster didn't hit the walls of the first courthouse until May of the following year. It took another three months for a trial to happen there.

Since that time, the Courthouse has changed a lot—major extensions happened in 1871, 1913, and 1930, and it's been remodeled many more times. But one thing hasn't changed: All of the major legal judgments in Delaware County have passed through here. That means that it is a monument to high-minded legal thinking— and also a place where serious crimes, strange legal cases, and a parade of all the dumb criminals of Delco come together.

We know a lot of serious work takes place here, but we are going to focus just on a few of the strange or macabre cases that have been heard here.

But before we get started, we are often asked whether there are any ghosts in the Courthouse. We always used to answer "no," but we had to change that answer when a security guard there came up to a Media Gothic tour group ready to move us along. (Remember: Media's loitering ordinances of 1870 and 1876 forbade groups of two or more from blocking sidewalks in the Borough).

When he heard what we were doing, he casually mentioned "You know this place is haunted, don't you?" and went on to tell us the details. Between the hours of 11 o'clock at night to around 1 AM, security guards are often disturbed by the sound of footsteps around the judge's chambers. Nobody has discovered a source for these sounds or for the faint echo of a young girl laughing that often accompanies the footsteps. We don't know why a child's ghost would haunt the judge's chambers, but apparently, one does.

MEDIA COURT HOUSE IN 1875 AND NOW

DIGGING UP A SERIAL KILLER

One of the oddest stories to hit the news in recent years started, strangely enough, with a petition to the Delaware County Orphan's Court in the Media Courthouse, back in the spring of 2017. The story started out strangely, with a request from a Nevada resident to dig up and remove the body of his great-great-grandfather from the Holy Cross Catholic cemetery in Yeadon. But it only gets stranger from there.

The petitioner wanted to excavate the unmarked grave of his relative, have the bones removed for forensic study, and to rebury them later in the same spot. He also wanted to film the excavation for a documentary to air on the History Channel. Oh, and the great-great-grandfather in question was H. H. Holmes, a notorious Victorian serial killer whose fame had spread a century after his death because he was the subject of an award-winning nonfiction book called *The Devil in the White City* by Erik Larson.

In the Media courthouse Orphan's Court, presiding judge Chad Kenney heard that newspapers in 1896, the year Holmes was executed in Philadelphia, suggested that he may have escaped the gallows and substituted another body for burial. The petitioner, a writer named Jeff Mudgett, believed that exhumation and forensic study would prove once and for all if that printed rumor was true. Though such requests are rare, the Orphan's Court is exactly where you go to get permission to do this, so Justice Kenney signed off on the request, but he made some strict rules about how the job should be done. Only a respected organization should be allowed to conduct the exhumation. Nobody except for expert contract workers, the family, security, and the documentary crew could be present. There was to be absolutely no "carnival atmosphere" at the cemetery during the exhumation or reburial.

The petitioner Jeff Mudgett had assembled a production team and had secured the services of experts from the Archaeology department at the University of Pennsylvania. The History Channel took care of the rest. You can see the results of their efforts in two episodes of the series American Ripper, in which Jeff Mudgett and a former FBI profiler named Amaryllis Fox try to prove that H. H. Holmes was also the notorious London killer Jack the Ripper.

If all this seems macabre and strange, pace yourself because this story gets a lot weirder. News reports from 1896 say that Holmes was executed by hanging in Moyamensing Prison in south Philadelphia and his body turned over to an undertaker for burial in Holy Cross Cemetery, about five miles from the site of the execution.

This was no ordinary burial. Holmes had sold his story as a book and as a printed confession in the newspapers, and he had netted a huge amount of money for it: More than $7,500 in 1890s dollars. He used some of this money to arrange a strange burial. He wanted his hanged body lain in a large box—not a regular coffin—half-full of wet cement. Once he had sunk into the mixture, he wanted the box topped up with more wet cement. After the mix had hardened, he wanted to be buried ten feet deep in an unmarked grave in consecrated ground. Just like Media's hanged felons Albert West and "Kid" Jones, he was apparently terrified that his body would be cut up and examined after his death (something he knew about from personal experience as a doctor—and murderer.)

A century later, Holmes's great-great-grandson—with the assistance of the History Channel, the University of Pennsylvania, and Media's Orphan's Court—had his body dug up and examined, the very thing that Holmes had feared. UPenn archaeologists located the cement-filled box, chipped it open, found the bones, and removed them all, leaving the cement and clothes behind.

For an entire summer, they compared the skeleton to records of Holmes's body size, shape, and dental records. They drilled into the back of his skull to remove bone dust for DNA comparison to Holmes's descendants. And nobody found out the results until they aired on the final episode of American Ripper. The weight of forensic evidence pointed to the inescapable conclusion that the body buried in Yeadon was indeed the body of H. H. Holmes, the notorious Chicago serial killer.

But, of course, no story this weird will ever end tidily. In one final strange twist, the great-great-grandson of the killer wasn't satisfied with the findings. He has been trying ever since all this took place, back in 2017, to re-open the case, and indeed the grave. If that ever happens, it will once again have to go through the Media courthouse.

THE FLASH BANDIT

One of the more colorful characters to pass through the Courthouse was a charismatic armed robber named Clifford Redden, better known to his fan base (and yes, he had a fan base) as the Flash Bandit. In a relatively brief crime spree, he committed 69 armed robberies, stole 29 cars, and crossed a whole continent to avoid capture—sending picture postcards back to Delco's lawmen with a teasing signature "Wish you were here—Your Pal, Flash."

Like many veterans of World War Two, Cliff Redden returned from service to his wife and children—and no job. With little to recommend him except a clean war record, a ninth grade education, and a Luger handgun taken as a souvenir from a German soldier, he had few options. The one he chose was armed robbery, and he took to his new job with professional zeal.

Wearing his trademark sunglasses, he would hit up to six establishments per night along Chester Pike or MacDade Boulevard. He zipped in, took money, and zipped out, sometimes handing a banknote from his pocket as a parting gift to a sales clerk he had just robbed.

He once flipped a quarter at a child who had witnessed one of his robberies.

These quaint gestures may have endeared him to readers of the *Chester Times* (the newspaper that morphed into the *Delaware County Daily Times*), but they did not sit at all well with law enforcement. And when the assistant manager at one of the places he had robbed recognized the man behind the sunglasses, things got too hot for Redden in his stamping ground. He hit the road, first to New York and then all the way across the country to California, committing armed robberies all the way. The self-confessed thrill seeker picked up a small fortune along the way, and was living a playboy's life in San Diego when he confided in a new acquaintance how he had made his fortune. The acquaintance reported him to the authorities, and he was extradited back to Media to stand trial.

Presiding over the proceedings was Judge Albert MacDade, the county's former District Attorney and the man they named MacDade Boulevard after. MacDade was not lenient. He sentenced Redden to between ten and twenty years per crime he had committed in Judge MacDade's jurisdiction—and that was a total of 39 crimes.

I SURVIVED ALCATRAZ TWICE
by Clifford R. Redden

America's Notorious
FLASH BANDIT

So with a total of 400-plus years in sentences, Redden began his new life as a convict.

But Redden was a model prisoner, and he was released in the mid-1950s after serving a fraction of his sentence. But ten years of crime and punishment hadn't increased his chances of gainful employment, so by 1957, Redden took another stab at making a quick buck in a West Philadelphia bank. Witnesses had a good look at his face, but there was another person in the area who looked quite a bit like him, and it was the lookalike who got arrested and charged.

Clifford R. Redden was many things, but he was a man of honor, and he felt guilty about another man being blamed for his crime. So he hit upon a way of getting his doppelganger off—he would commit the same crime in the same area in the same way. With the other guy locked up, the police would know he was innocent and let him go.

The plan worked like a charm—for the other guy. Cliff, however, got arrested and had the book thrown at him once again. After his conviction, he spent time in Eastern State Penitentiary, Leavenworth, and did two stints in San Francisco's Alcatraz.

When he was finally released, he renounced his former thrill-seeking crime-committing ways. He lived out the rest of his life in a variety of honest blue-collar pursuits in Delaware County, and collaborated with a local journalist in a 1995 biography—*I Survived Alcatraz Twice*—which is out of print but can still be found if you look hard enough.

MURDER AND MADNESS

Not all the cases that came before the court in Media have charismatic criminals who reform themselves and live happily ever after. One of the darker and more notorious cases that crossed the docket here was that of John E. du Pont, a wealthy heir from Newtown Square, whose descent into madness became the subject of the 2013 Steve Carrell movie Foxcatcher. It involved paranoia, delusions, and murder, and one of the more protracted court proceedings in Pennsylvania history.

In January of 1996, du Pont drove through his estate, Foxcatcher Farms, to a house occupied by the coach of the Olympic wrestling team that had been training on the premises for years. He rolled down the window and when coach Dave Schultz approached, Du Pont shot him with a .357 Magnum revolver, shouted "You got a problem with me?" and shot him twice more. Then he drove back to the mansion house at the heart of his estate, told his secretary "If the police show up, don't let them in," and barricaded himself in for a siege.

The SWAT team knew how heavily armed du Pont was, because he had let them train on Foxcatcher's shooting range, and they had seen what kind of an arsenal he was packing. So they weren't about to knock on his door and burst in. They called him on the phone instead. They got very little sense and no cooperation from him, so there was a two-day standoff. Eventually, the authorities cut the power to the mansion, and ambushed du Pont as he slinked out of the building to fix the heating.

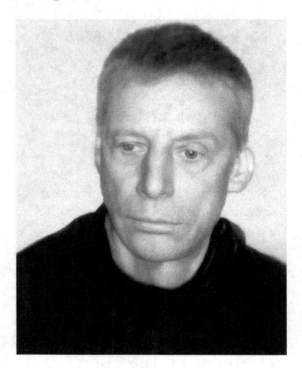

John du Pont around the time of his arrest

At this point, the story took on two separate narratives. As far as the prosecution was concerned, du Pont was upset with Schultz. Dave had confided to his employer that he planned to quit Team Foxcatcher after the 1996 Olympics, and take up a coaching position out of state. After mulling this bad news for a few days, du Pont flew into a jealous rage, and killed Dave in the kind of spoiled-child tantrum that can be summed up with the sentiment "If I can't have him, nobody can!"

As far as the defense was concerned, du Pont had built an elaborate fantasy world in which Schultz represented an enemy of the United States. In his own twisted way, killing Schultz was the only logical thing to do.

The only thing that the prosecution and defense could both agree on was the obvious one: John du Pont was clearly out of his mind.

But it was only after his arrest that the extent of his illness became clear. He fired his defense attorneys after a few months because he was convinced they were conspiring to kill him. His new attorney Thomas Bergstrom successfully petitioned for a competency hearing, but by September 1996 had publicly stated that he had still not successfully completed a coherent conversation with his client.

"John's delusional system, his paranoia, was in full bloom," Bergstrom said, "It was impossible to communicate with this man. The first problem I had was ethically trying to determine how can I possibly represent this man who hasn't a clue as to why I'm here, why he is where he is, and what are we gonna do about all this.

"The problem with John was that John believed that he was a prisoner of war, and that the military should take over and try this case. And he would be exonerated because of his status as a prisoner of war."

It took months of psychological treatment in the forensic unit at Norristown State Hospital, building 51, before John was deemed competent to stand trial. He had been medicated with Haldol for the duration of his stay ("somewhat against his will," in his attorney's words).

The trial began about a year after the crime occurred, in late January 1997.

"This was not a whodunit," said Bergstrom, "There was never any doubt in anybody's mind that John killed Dave Schultz. The question was "Why?""

"John didn't want to plead not guilty by reason of insanity. He did not want me to raise the insanity defense. John believed that Dave Schultz was a Russian agent, that the entire Soviet army would be in Newtown Square, and that there would be the war of all wars. That John's property was holy ground. That John alternated between being Jesus Christ, the Dalai Lama, and the last heir to the Russian throne. Up to the time that he died, he believed that he had to kill Schultz because Schultz was going to kill him."

"So the delusions that danced in his head continued," Bergstrom said, "He was so delusional and so paranoid that he had Pat Goodale his security guard, and his agents, literally install barbed wire inside the walls of his house, because he thought that people were crawling around inside the walls. He dug tunnels under the house to find the people who were trying to get into the walls of the house. That was John du Pont.

"It's hard to convince a jury of twelve people to find "not guilty by reason of insanity," because the jury believes "if we do that, he's going to wander out some day and kill somebody else, so they are loath to find that verdict. After Hinckley shot Reagan in the early 80s, most legislatures in this country passed a bill that permitted "guilty but mentally ill," and that's the compromise verdict we got."

With a verdict like that, John du Pont could have been sentenced to between 20 and 30 years; he was actually sentenced to 13 years. He went to Crescent State Prison in the middle of the state, where he stayed, medicated and treated, for almost the entire length of his sentence.

To this day, his attorney believed this crime could have been avoided.

"All John needed was that therapy and that medication. Would he have rejected it? Yes, early on, but when the medication takes hold, we saw it in the case…John got better. Did he get well? No. Was he ever going to be well? No. But he got better."

"I think that if John's mother had lived, none of this would have happened. She paid for a friend to monitor him and watch him. When she passed away the bottom fell out of things. His mother was gone. His friend was gone. There were all these people who were feeding his paranoia with the barbed wire and the razor wire and the tunnels. And guns, and everything else. It was awful. Awful. There was no doubt what was going to happen. It was inevitable. Fifty caliber machine guns on tanks. It was nuts!"

As it was, John du Pont reached the age of 72 on November 22, 2000, medicated in jail in Somerset County. He was awaiting the end of his sentence, but on December 9th, two weeks before the shortest day of winter, he died. Not long after that, the estate was pulled down to build luxury houses. You can drive past them on 252; they are the Lisiter Farms complex on the left as you head north between West Chester Pike and Lancaster Pike.

In the process of pulling down the estate, the demolition experts destroyed a chilling piece of evidence of John du Pont's obsession with guns. At the end of the Olympic-sized swimming pool he maintained for the wrestling team, he had, years before, commissioned a huge mural showing the five sports in the Modern Pentathlon. There was a freestyle swimmer, a horse rider doing show jumping, a fencer, a cross-country runner, and finally, a man holding a pistol. These represent the five disciplines in the modern pentathlon, but there was a creepy and ominous quirk to this particular mural. The marksman with the pistol was pointing it towards the fencer.

It was a mural showing an Olympic sportsman pointing a gun at another Olympic sportsman. And everyone on the wrestling team trained with this image facing them for years before it became a chilling reality.

Detail of the mural on the wall of Foxcatcher Farm's Olympic swimming pool, now demolished. Taken by team Media Gothic before its demolition.

HIGH MICE AND MISDEMEANORS

Although this next story never made the newspapers, it's widely whispered among newspaper reporters and was repeated in Jack Myers' book The Delco Files without a source or dates. With that caveat in mind, brace yourselves for a story that we can't prove is true, but which has been repeated often enough behind closed doors that it's worth repeating one more time.

There was a drug bust in Delaware County that netted a sizeable quantity of marijuana—clearly too much for personal use, so the prosecution decided to charge the hapless suspect with possession of a controlled substance with intent to sell. (Being convicted as a drug dealer carries harsher penalties than mere possession of narcotics.)

The drugs were impounded and secured in an evidence storeroom in the courthouse. The trial date was set, and the District Attorney's office assembled a team and a strategy for prosecuting the case. As the date of the trial approached, they put in a request to retrieve the evidence and to submit it into evidence for the imminent trial.

But it had gone missing.

No matter how hard the officers of the court looked, they could find no trace of the big bag of weed the police had impounded during the arrest. Without evidence, the trial could not be prosecuted, so the DA's office was forced to drop the case.

The best excuse that any of the people responsible for taking care of evidence could muster was this: There had been an infestation of mice in the court buildings, and maybe—just maybe—they had eaten the evidence.

It's hard to tell whether this response was supposed to be taken seriously—but most people who repeat this story find it hard to stifle a smirk. However, with no smoking gun, so to speak, the matter was quietly dropped.

As far-fetched as this excuse sounds, it is not the only time that law enforcement has used this explanation: As recently as 2018, an Argentinian police precinct claimed mice had destroyed a truly colossal haul of half a ton of marijuana.

Next to that, the alleged Delco courthouse losses seem…weedy.

MOST CONTEMPTIBLE

Before we start to make too much fun of the Media courthouse, it's worth bearing one thing in mind: The judges here can be extremely strict. As a case in point, the longest incarceration for contempt of court in the history of the United States originated right here in Media in the 1990s.

It was a divorce case between a high-powered lawyer from a Philadelphia law firm and his much younger second wife. The marriage had crumbled because of irreconcilable differences, and the wife wanted out. The husband, H. Beatty Chadwick, was attempting to plead poverty to prevent his soon-to-be ex-wife from walking away from the marriage with a tidy settlement.

Chadwick's reputation as a bit of a Scrooge had came out in the divorce papers—he had been giving his wife a small allowance and expected her to run their large and pristine house with it, and he micromanaged every aspect of her life until she couldn't take it anymore. When she sued for divorce, Chadwick dropped a bombshell: He said that his entire net worth of $2.7 million

dollars had vanished in a bad overseas investment in Gibraltar.

This story didn't have the ring of truth to it, so the courts demanded a full accounting of Chadwick's assets. Then they demanded it again. And again. And H. Beatty Chadwick ignored each request. So the court ruled he was in contempt and put him in jail until he provided the paperwork they demanded.

That was in 1995. He stayed in jail until 2009. That's fourteen years in jail. Without a conviction. Without a trial. Without even a criminal charge. And guy in the cell was a lawyer!

The only reason they finally released him is this: They came to the conclusion that if a man spends his entire 60s in jail without cooperating, he won't suddenly start cooperating when he's 70-something years old. Or, to use Judge Joseph Cronin's words, "Chadwick's incarceration had lost its coercive effect."

So if any Media judges are reading this, please be aware we aren't holding you in any contempt when we wonder about how mice could destroy large amounts of evidence in your workplace.

Honestly.

After 25 years of progressive and thoughtful development in Media, Mr. Philip Green, President of Philip Green & Co., Inc., and Delaware County Mortgage & Finance Co., Inc., is realizing his dream to erect a modern six (6) story office and apartment building on the S. W. Cor. of Front and South Avenue, opposite our magnificent Delaware County Court House.

The architect's painting, a portion of which you see above, represents 25 years of industrious development for the betterment of the borough of Media.

Heretofore Philip Green & Co., Inc., and associates have renovated and modernized a great many of the extremely old buildings in Media at a tremendous cost and a great investment to them.

The County Building, which is a modernized five (5) story office and apartment building on the S. E. Cor. of Front and South Avenue, opposite the Court House, was formerly known as Gleave Hall and is known to be 100 years old or more.

Plymouth Hall, which is now a modern apartment building on the S. W. Cor. of South Avenue and Jasper Street, was formerly known as Charter House and is also over 100 years old.

The present Penn State Building, which is a magnificent structure, consisting of stores and offices, was formerly the old Media Title and Trust Company Bank.

Philip Green & Co., Inc., and associates have also developed and modernized the S. E. Cor. of State and Olive Streets, which now consists of the Esquire Shop and six (6) apartments.

They have also developed the adjacent property, which is a modern new store and six (6) apartments building.

They have recently completed the erection of a new building, consisting of the Sherwin-Williams Paint Store and six (6) apartments situate at No. 31 W. State Street, adjacent to the new building they are in the process of completing and modernizing; the N. W. Cor. of State and Plum Streets, which will consist of five (5) magnificent modern stores and eleven (11) modern apartments. They have also developed the N. E. Cor. of State and South Avenue, which is now the State Cut Rate Drug Company and the Norma Apartments.

Philip Green & Co. and associates have also recently completed forty-eight (48) modern semi-detached stone and brick dwellings in the vicinity of Providence Road, State Road and Greenhill Road, which is known as the Green Hill Manor Development. In the same area, they are presently developing a group of forty-eight (48) apartments. Numerous tracts of ground owned by Philip Green Associates in and surrounding the Media area are also being planned for development within a short time which will considerably increase the population and the drawing capacity of the Borough of Media.

The future plans of Philip Green & Co., Inc., and associates are many and varied and with the foremost thought of developing and modernizing Media to make it "THE NUMBER ONE TOWN ON THE NUMBER ONE HIGHWAY."

PHILIP GREEN and COMPANY, Inc.

County Building   **Media, Pa.**

THE COUNTY BUILDING

As Media's centennial celebration approached in 1950, one of the Borough's most prominent developers, Philip Green, hatched an ambitious building scheme. He wanted to construct a six-story mixed-use building—part residential apartment building, part office block—right opposite the Courthouse. He even took out a full-page ad in the Media Centennial book with an artist's impression of how the County Building would look, right there the southwest corner of Front Street and what was then called South Avenue (now Veteran's Square).

Philip Green also took the opportunity in this ad to brag about all the great work his company had done in remodeling such Media landmarks as the Charter House hotel—which he turned into Plymouth Hall residential apartments—and the entire southeastern corner of State and Olive Streets. At the end of this volley of self-congratulation, the copywriter built up to a crescendo that shouted the town's mid-century motto in all capital letters:

THE NUMBER ONE TOWN ON THE NUMBER ONE HIGHWAY.

(It wasn't until much later that Media became America's First Fair Trade Town and Everybody's Hometown.)

Somewhere along the line, Philip Green & Company was denied planning permission to build a building taller than the Courthouse right opposite the Courthouse, but a shorter version of the proposed building did go up.

It only took two decades for the County Building to become notorious.

It became the epicenter of a scandal that undermined a Federal government agency. It also gave the building a new unofficial name: the FBI Building.

COUNTY BUILDING – 50 YEARS AFTER THE SCANDAL

COINTELPRO CRUMBLES

The Federal Bureau of Investigation was a minor presence in Media for a few years until the early 1970s. They rented a two-room branch office in the County Building at 1 Veterans Square, but even though they have been gone for fifty years, everybody in the know still refers to the place as the FBI Building. That's because of what went down one night in 1971, and the ripples that were felt through the world in the months and years that followed.

The night was March 8th, and most of the nation was watching a prizefight between boxing heavyweights Joe Frazier and Muhammad Ali. The result of that heavily touted battle would probably have dominated the news for the rest of the week, except for something that happened in room 204 of the County Building in Media that night.

Before their crime had even been noticed, the conspirators had already claimed responsibility. In the early hours of the next morning, they phoned in a news release from a callbox to the Reuters news service.

This is was what they said:

On the night of March 8, 1971, the Citizens' Commission to Investigate the FBI removed files from the Media, Pennsylvania, office of the FBI. These files will now be studied to determine:

One, the nature and extent of surveillance and intimidation carried on by this office of the FBI, particularly against groups and individuals working for a more just, humane and peaceful society.

Two, to determine how much of the FBI's efforts are spent on relatively minor crimes by the poor and the powerless against whom they can get a more glamorous conviction rate. Instead of investigating truly serious crimes by those with money and influence which cause great damage to the lives of many people—crimes such as war profiteering, monopolistic practices, institutional racism, organized crime, and the mass distribution of lethal drugs.

Finally, three, the extent of illegal practices by the FBI, such as eavesdropping, entrapment, and the use of provocateurs and informers.

As this study proceeds, the results obtained along with the FBI documents pertaining to them will be sent to people in public life who have demonstrated the integrity, courage and commitment to democratic *values which are necessary to effectively challenge the repressive policies of the FBI.*

As long as the United States government wages war against Indochina in defiance of the vast majority who want all troops and weapons withdrawn this year, and extends that war and suffering under the guise of reducing it. As long as great economic and political power remains concentrated in the hands of a small clique not subject to democratic scrutiny and control. Then repression, intimidation, and entrapment are to be expected. We do not believe that this destruction of democracy and democratic society results simply from the evilness, egoism or senility of some leaders. Rather, this destruction is the result of certain undemocratic social, economic and political institutions.

In the polarized political climate of Vietnam-era America, this manifesto would have been easy to dismiss as the act of radicals, or even domestic terrorists. But in the weeks that followed, this group of burglar/activists made good on their promise to deliver evidence that the FBI was overstepping its authority, and even breaking the law. The Bureau had been acting on an internal initiative called Cointelpro, the Counter Intelligence Program, for the past 15 years. The internal memos showed that this program targeted a wide range of groups they believed were engaged in un-American activities, but a simple count of the files showed that they were largely focused on women's liberation groups, black activists, antiwar protesters, and, to quote one memo, "hippie types."

Only 1 percent of the FBI's files were devoted to organized crime; 14 percent concerned military desertion and draft dodging—the same number of files as they kept for all the bank robberies, interstate thefts, and murders in the United States. A full 40 percent of the files fell under the category of political surveillance—and it was blatantly biased surveillance: There were only two cases kept on right-wing groups, ten files on immigrants, and more than 200 on suspected leftist groups—including such unlikely organizations as the Boy Scouts. Skewed priorities and political bias weren't the only problem with the FBI's approach. Their stated goal in the words of one memo was to "enhance the paranoia endemic in these circles," and "to get the point across there is an FBI agent behind every mailbox."

To that end, they skirted surveillance laws by using wiretap recordings to blackmail such civil rights luminaries as Martin Luther King. They had a strategy of planting fabricated news stories that would discredit or cause arguments among their political opponents. And according to the first 14 documents sent to the *Washington Post*, the Bureau had recruited a local police chief, letter carriers and a college switchboard operator to eavesdrop on and observe campus groups in the Philadelphia area.

Even the most respected commentator in the country, Walter Cronkite, a scrupulously fair news anchor whose nickname was The Most Trusted Man in America, dismissed the Bureau's approach as "snooping on civilians" in evening news broadcasts.

The FBI director J. Edgar Hoover was publicly embarrassed and furious. He detailed 200 agents to devote the next five years to trying to find the people responsible for the burglary in Media, until the statute of limitations ran out on the crime. They built up a 33,000-page file on the case, couldn't solve it.

The only action Hoover could take was to make sure this didn't happen again— so he closed down the Media office and about 500 other small bureaus with inadequate security.

That would be the end of the story, but more than forty years after the burglaries took place, when one of the newspaper reporters who broke the story was writing a book on the subject, several of the burglars came forward. Six of the eight members of the group identified themselves to reporter Betty Medsger, and were interviewed in depth for her 2014 book *The Burglary: The Discovery of J. Edgar Hoover's Secret F.B.I.*

The conspirators who revealed themselves were a motley crew: college professors, a cab driver, and a daycare operator. And their legacy went beyond perpetrating a daring burglary, and keeping quiet about it for four decades.

In the words of a *Los Angeles Times* article from forty years later, the publication of these documents "remains one of the most lastingly consequential (although underemphasized) watersheds of political awareness in recent American history, one that poses tough questions even today for our national leaders who argue that fighting foreign enemies requires the government to spy on its citizens."

And it all started here in Media, opposite the courthouse.

SECTION 3
A STROLL DOWN STATE STREET

1899: NEW BANK, ALREADY HAUNTED.

A STROLL DOWN STATE STREET

The stretch of State Street from the old First National Bank of Media down to the Media Elementary School is just a few blocks. It's less than half a mile. But it's packed with two centuries worth of strange history—and if you can believe the dozens of people we've interviewed, it's also home to more than a few ghosts.

This part of the book focuses on just ten addresses along this stretch of road, but it includes cases of fire, gunfire, insane killers, a bewildering number of ghosts, and one giant explosion.

So stand outside the bank building (better known to locals as "the Castle"), take a leisurely stroll down the street, and just feel the history soak in. Along the way, you'll walk past quite a few shops and restaurants, so here's a few Media bucks for you to spend on the way.

The First National Bank of Media had a charter to issue its own currency, which it did until 1935. It produced nearly $4 million worth of nationally legal currency, including this five-dollar bill.

FIRST NATIONAL BANK OF MEDIA, WITH GHOST – 1898

114 WEST STATE STREET

"The Castle" was built to impress. The year was 1899, and Media's most successful bank had been thriving for 35 years. As Media's 50th anniversary—the Semi-Centennial—loomed, the bank really needed to expand.

The First National Bank building, operating as PNC Bank in 2011.

Its name—The First National Bank of Media—sounded imposing, but this was a bank with humble origins. Its first offices were on the second floor of Haldeman's grocery store down the road, and the business had bounced from modest building to modest building at various corners of this intersection for many years since.

As the century was ending, the bank was thriving, taking in deposits of half a million dollars every month, and any financial institution that successful needed a suitably grand setting.

The directors were not going to do anything by half-measures. They commissioned an imposing granite castle with turrets and arches and a big bronze gate. What they didn't foresee was that like all castles, the bank would end up being haunted.

Detail from the left part of the First National Bank's President's Room photograph shown opposite. Do you see the transparent man?

The Media Bank Ghost is something of a local legend. It has been seen and its presence felt by many people in living memory, but its most famous manifestation shows up in an 1898 photograph taken in the old bank building on this site.

At the end of an array of paneled teller stations in this picture is the open door to the President's Room. And there in the room is the transparent image of an impressive-looking fellow, looking every inch the bank president he probably was.

At this point in history, the bank's first two presidents had died—so is this the specter of Isaac Haldeman, the founder and first president, who died in 1878? Or is it his son and successor, Thomas J. Haldeman, who died in 1894? Or is it a photographic image of the then-living president, Joseph Hawley, who noticed the cameraman at work in his bank and walked away while the photo was half-exposed, leaving part of his image on film and allowing the background to show through after he left?

Nobody can say for sure—the transparent image shows too little of the face to make a positive identification. But to generations of Media's ghost-seeking residents, this photograph stands as evidence of paranormal activity in the hub of Media's commercial district.

The First National Bank of Media's first president, Isaac Haldeman. Does this face look like the famous Media Bank Ghost to you?

Picture from Henry Ashmead's History of Delaware County.

115 WEST STATE STREET

There's something odd about the Phoenix Building. If you step through the arches then turn around and look up, you'll see. It looks like something took away all of a building except the front wall, and put another building ten feet behind it. Guess what? That's actually what happened.

The front wall is all that remains of Snowden's famous department store, established here in 1868. The building behind it rose from the company's ashes after disaster struck almost 120 years later. Snowden's was a mainstay of Media commerce, with its two massive display windows, one full of hardware, and another with whatever the management thought would bring the customers in. It was where you'd go for toys, collectibles, gifts, hardware, and necessities, and it was still going strong after more than a century, right up until Christmas, 1976.

The night after Christmas, Snowden's caught fire. The blaze started a little before 7pm in the back of the building, and swept rapidly through the store. As it raged into the night, firefighters feared for the buildings around it. This wasn't a mere four-alarm fire. It was a seven-alarmer, and intensity of the fire combined with the thick black smoke and sub-zero weather made it tough to manage.

As workers from the Federal Savings Bank braved the building next door to retrieve computers and paperwork, fire trucks pointed a snorkel boom at the flames and rained cold water on Snowden's from a height. At one point, captured in a blurry photograph and later printed on the front page of the *Delaware County Daily Times*, the boom touched the trolley power lines, sending arcs of electricity from the truck and causing the firemen to scatter.

By the following day, the Snowden building was in ruins and the buildings next to it were damaged by heat and water. Only the front wall was intact, and it was covered with hundreds of icicles from the previous night's dousing. The company decided not to reopen, so a multi-office complex was built to replace it. The new building honored its predecessor: It retained Snowden's distinctive façade, and took a new name, Phoenix, after the mythical bird that rises from its own ashes.

Delaware County
Daily Times

HOME DELIVERY 75 CENTS   MOTOR ROUTE 90 CENTS

Thursday, December 30, 1976

PRICE: FIFTEEN CENTS

Snowden's struck by fire

Department store a Media landmark

...RAY
f Writer

ouncil Wed-
hat it will
e policemen
eat of a tax
the recently
act.
acrelli said
50,000 more
n allocated
l budget of

ncrease in
led, would
f 3 mills or
ssed valua-

ouncil went
Wednesday
oudget that
nt tax rate
s per $1,000

no tax in-
d after the
review the
atever steps
e tax rate
will mean a
onnel."

id council
w the situa-
g just how
e their jobs.
y that "we
department
ection with

e protected
acrelli said,
be carried
y.
ent's 140

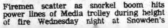
Firemen scatter as snorkel boom hits power lines of Media trolley during height of fire Wednesday night at Snowden's department store. Electrical flash can be seen beneath truck.

Photo by Paul Layman

MEDIA — A more than 100-year-old department store was extensively damaged by a six alarm fire Wednesday night.

Flames leaped from the four-story Snowden's department store at 117 State St. as the fire raged out of control for more than two hours.

Spectators lined the borough's streets to watch firemen battle the blaze which broke out just before 7 p.m., but the billowing black smoke and sub-freezing temperatures soon sent most inside.

There were no reported injuries in the fire. The store had been closed when the fire started somewhere in the rear of the building.

Fire Chief Robert Hazlett said a first-story rear floor collapsed, for a time preventing firemen from getting to the area where the fire apparently began.

The cause of the blaze was not immediately determined. Hazlett estimated damages at more than $500,000.

First Federal Savings and Loan Association, which is next door, received some water damage, the chief said. Records and computers were removed from the savings and loan building as a precaution.

President Edmund Jones said this morning the savings and loan would open for business as usual today in temporary headquarters at 216 W. State St.

Traffic was rerouted for a

Next Feb. 1, Snowden's Department Store would have celebrated 109 years in business.

Samuel Hawley started the original general merchandise store in Media three days after Abraham Lincoln was assassinated.

Horseshoes, nails, buggy whips, groceries and farm implements were the mainstay of Hawley's business in those days when Media was still a village.

Twenty-one years after the opening a new clerk was hired. A diligent worker and fast learner, Henry Snowden started as a general handyman, swept floors, waited on customers before becoming the store's bookkeeper.

Hawley was so impressed with the younger Snowden, he changed the painted sign outside to read "Hawley and Snowden" and a new partnership was formed.

When Hawley died in 1905, Snowden acquired the controlling stock and became the owner. Snowden died in 1936.

several block area. The Southeastern Pennsylvania Transporation Authority's Media trolley line was also interrupted by the fire. Trolleys from 69th

See SNOWDEN'S, Page

113 WEST STATE STREET

Sligo Irish Pub is not the first bar to operate at 113 West State Street, but like its predecessors, it has strange quirks that throw back to Media's origins as a temperance town. From Media's inception clear up until the 1930s, it was against local laws to buy, sell, or consume alcohol anywhere in the Borough. Seventy years after Media's temperance ordinances, the entire nation joined in the anti-drink trend when the 18th Amendment to the Constitution to prohibited alcohol anywhere in the U.S.

It wasn't till 1933, when the 21st Amendment repealed Prohibition, that Media allowed intoxicating spirits within the Borough limits. But Pennsylvania wasn't about to make it easy: Liquor licenses were not—and still aren't—easy to get. One of the easier ways to get permission to sell liquor was to operate a hotel. And that's why the top floor of Sligo has a number of bedrooms—tiny closet-sized rooms just big enough to fit a twin bed. This technically makes the business a hotel, and eligible for one of the easier-to-get liquor licenses.

But don't expect to rent a room for the night: it has not operated as a hotel in living memory, and as far as our researches can tell, it never did.

And yet there's a persistent bar story about these rooms that some people consider the origin of the ghost that haunts the upper rooms of Sligo.

The story goes that someone who had been drinking all night decided to go upstairs and sleep it off. He slipped into one of the front bedrooms and collapsed in a drunken heap for a good night's sleep. The problem was, he never woke up. Normally, if you die in your sleep in a hotel, someone will come looking for you, or the cleaning staff will find you. But nobody knew he'd ventured upstairs that night, and that part of the building wasn't used very often. So it was a while before they stumbled upon him, and what they found wasn't a pretty sight.

We've not been able to find any news stories to back up this story, but people do sometimes experience paranormal activity at Sligo—mostly in the second floor event room. It's nothing scary or threatening—people sometimes get jostled by an unseen person, or feel a hand on their arm or shoulder, or see their drinks move across the table. It's just the kind of behavior you'd expect from a happy drunkard, as he staggers away to sleep off a night's drink.

110 WEST STATE STREET

Kenny's Flower Shoppe has been a fixture in Media for more than 40 years. Over that time, it has gained a good reputation for providing beautiful floral arrangements and great customer service. Times change, and management changes, but that reputation lives on. A hundred years ago, you could say exactly the same thing about the business at this address, but it was a very different type of business back then. Yes, there were flower arrangements, but they were only a small part of the original business of the building—arranging funerals.

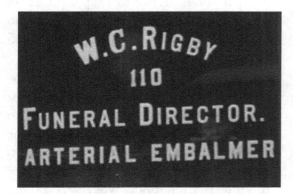

Detail from a picture from about 1900. You can see the whole thing on page 59. Do you see the small child peeking out over the word EMBALMER?

W. C. Rigby, Funeral Director and Arterial Embalmer, inherited the business from his father and built a great reputation about town. He served on the Borough Council and belonged to businessmen's associations. He would lend his fine white horses to the local fire brigade for special occasions like parades and fairs. On more than one occasion, having these ringers on the team enabled the Media Hook & Ladder No. 1 to take home prizes from parade judges. And it was all down to William C. Rigby.

You'd expect a building that used to revolve around the business of death to have ghost stories, and sure enough, there are a few.

A couple who lived in one of the upstairs apartments reported something strange that used to happen on a very precise schedule. Between 3 and 3:30 every afternoon, their cat would alert on a particular corner—a blank area with no doors—reach up, and scratch away at it. No more than 20 minutes later, the cat would lose interest and walk away. This routine was so regular and inexplicable, the couple believed that either the walls had very punctual mice, or something paranormal was taking place.

But that is not the only strange thing that happened repeatedly in the upstairs apartments. The husband saw a woman out of the corner of his eye; a blonde who seemed tall and stern, and wore an old-fashioned sack dress. It reminded him of a pilgrim. There was something else that seemed unusual but he didn't have time to take it in because the apparition vanished. Like so many of us, he shrugged the vision off as an overactive imagination. Except that the next time he saw her, he figured out what the unusual thing was that he'd not noticed before. Her hands were clasped in front of her, with her elbows at right angles, with one hand over the other, and the fingers of each hand hooked around each other. Once again he shrugged it off—until a few days later, when his wife confided in him that she'd seen something strange in the flat. It was a tall blonde dressed like a pilgrim, with her hands clasped like a choir singer.

Some of Kenny's staff also have tales of mischievous paranormal activity in the workplace. Contractors doing renovation work have told the manager that someone messes with their tools overnight, and sometimes things go astray during the workday too. Security cameras that were pointing at doors when the store closed will be facing the wall by morning.

Some of the regular staff have taken control of the situation by talking in a friendly way to whatever's pulling these stunts. The rationale is that if you thank a supernatural force for keeping the store safe while the security cameras are facing the wall, you bring the spirit onto the team. And according to one stone-cold serious report, this seems to work. One person we interviewed who worked at Kenny's told us that as she was closing the door with a large and cumbersome arrangement in her arms, she realized she had left a light on. As she was saying goodbye to the empty room (a good habit if you're trying to keep a ghost on your side), she asked for help. "Can you take care of that for me?" she called … and the light went out.

Next time you walk past Kenny's, here's a fun thing to ponder: When it was Rigby's funeral home, they used to store bodies in a cool recess in the basement called a cadaver shelf. It looks something like a pizza oven. This secret morgue is right under your feet as you pass by the front door of Kenny's.

It's now used to store Christmas decorations.

21-25 WEST STATE STREET

Before it became three separate stores, the three addresses on the northwest corner of State and Plum Streets were occupied by one big market. It was part of a small chain of stores that began in South Philly called the American Store, but it soon took on the name it's still known by today: Acme.

and moved to five storefront addresses up the road—315-323 State Street—before ultimately moving out to Baltimore Pike.

Somewhere along the line, this address picked up some paranormal activity. People who work in the retail and food service businesses there know it and when they are not busy with customers, may be prepared to tell you about it. But in some cases, they are too spooked to.

21-25 West State Street, a century ago.

21-25 West State Street, 2020.

Media's Acme Markets operated at this location until shortly before the Borough's centennial celebrations. By then the market had outgrown the space,

One of the common ways ghosts make their presence felt here is to move things around. Items rearrange themselves on the shelves—stuff that's typically set back in a staggered line will mysteriously move to the edge of a shelf in a dead straight line. Whatever does this has earned an affectionate nickname because of this habit: He's known as "the OCD ghost."

Food service businesses that have operated in this space have needed to be extra-vigilant about their equipment: their ovens tend to turn off by themselves during the workday—and sometimes turn on when the place is closed for the night.

On one occasion, things took an ugly turn when a piece of ceramic art spontaneously shattered in a store owner's hands. They began to burn sage in the store regularly after that—a precaution called smudging that is supposed to cleanse a space. (Sage smoke does not necessarily remove bacteria from the air, but smudging has been a common practice in Europe since Roman times, and also among Native Americans. It's believed to purify the air and to boost the mood and physical health of people in the space.)

And on one occasion, some kind of entity physically manifested itself: The owner of a business at this address saw a man lurking around the shelves, just standing there and looking, but not doing anything.

In other unpleasant news, the stairs to the basement in this row of businesses can be perilous—and not just because of structural issues. People seem to take a tumble down them more often than you'd think is normal. And all too often, the people who fall down the stairs there say that they did not stumble—they had a distinct feeling that they were being pushed or tripped.

But not every presence at this address is negative. Some are as helpful in death as they were in life. That seems to be the case with a handyman who used to be seen around the back of these businesses and those in the Plum Street pedestrian walkway back when he was alive.

He has been seen and his presence has been felt in the back areas of the stores since he died, in the workroom and the storage areas. He appears to have retained the same personality he had in life, and is a benign presence, happy enough to just let the employees know he is still there, taking care of and watching over the place and the people in it.

Sometimes a person likes their job so much they never want to leave it!

18 WEST STATE STREET

The Bryn Mawr Trust building is a bit of an anomaly. It's big—spreading from 16 to 22 West State Street—and Plum Street seems to avoid it. Plum Street stops across the street from its north side, and starts again at the far side of Baltimore Pike. That's because the original Plum Street used to plow straight through the place. This building is so big, it took over Plum Street on one side and the former Media post office on the other.

It's also the site of the biggest explosion ever to hit State Street.

The big bang went down late at night on 24 April, 1906, and its results were photographed by Media's resident photographer Stephen Horne Appleton. One of Appleton's crime-scene pictures appeared in the *Philadelphia Inquirer* the next day.

Apparently two or more burglars broke into the post office, located the safe, and planted high explosives under it. While they were ambitious, these burglars were clearly not Delco's smartest criminals. The Inquirer article calls them "yeggmen," a quaint Victorian term for burglar or safe-cracker, and under the headline "Wrecked Safe in Media Post Office," the article tells that they failed to steal anything that night. The charge peeled back the metal on the safe's outer door, spilling a lot of sand—the ballast that makes the safe heavy—but not cracking the safe's inner lining.

Not only did the yeggmen fail to steal anything, they apparently hadn't done much basic surveillance of the area before they set off a bomb in it. All the stores in that part of State Street had occupied apartments above them. Two young women who lived in one of them screamed at the sound of the explosion, and spooked the would-be thieves, who beat a hasty retreat. Empty-handed.

The interior of Media Post Office at the corner of Plum and State streets. Courtesy of the Media Historic Archives Commission.

POST OFFICE ROBBERY - EPIC FAIL

8356

2 WEST STATE STREET

If you look past the ultra-modernistic design of the storefront as it stands today, the building at 2 West State is the most Gothic place in all of Media. Built in the 1890s in the late Gothic style, its upper-story windows are all Gothic arches, and even some of its history has the dark and brooding madness we associate with Gothic literature.

Dark and brooding isn't how the building started out, though. It was constructed by a navy veteran and lawyer, John B. Robinson, to house his weekly newspaper, the *Media Ledger*. The *Ledger* was one of two weekly newspapers operating in Media at the time—the *Delaware County American* had been running for forty years, but the *Media Ledger* had an impetus that the older paper didn't: Political ambition. The *Ledger* lasted exactly as long as its owner's political career, which began in 1891 with a six-year term serving the Commonwealth as a Congressman in the Pennsylvania House of Representatives, and ended in 1913 after he retired from a succession of roles appointed by three U.S. presidents (McKinley, Teddy Roosevelt, and Taft).

After that point, the Media Ledger building was converted into a storefront with apartments upstairs, as it is today.

It was in this incarnation, a couple of world wars and most of a Cold War later, that the dark and brooding side of this building's Gothic nature would show up.

MEDIA HARDWARE

To anyone who grew up around Media in the 1980s, 2 West State Street was universally known as Media Hardware, a one-stop shop for appliances, tools, and home repair supplies. The upstairs floors were apartments, but downstairs was a hive of home-improvement activity. Many Media men who now have gray beards used to pick up shifts here as teenagers—including a couple of our sources for the next story.

The store was open from 7am to 6pm in the early 1980s, and teenage shift workers would try to grab parking spots as near to the front door as possible. One of them, a 17-year-old named Billy, parked a sporty little car he'd just bought right in front of the door to the apartments, and headed up to the store. He heard screaming and a splash behind him, and turned to see a young woman

in combat clothing who had just thrown her coffee all over his car. When he confronted her, he knew right away she was trouble—she had wild swiveling eyes and unleashed a stream of profanity at him—and she wasn't listening to reason.

In fact, she was listening to only one thing: The voices in her head, because she was a paranoid schizophrenic and she was off her meds. Even though he knew none of this, Billy knew something was wrong, so he backed off and headed into the store.

One of his school-age coworkers, Artie, knew who she was, and knew some of her story. Her name was Sylvia, she was in her early 20s, and she had lived in an apartment upstairs for a couple of years. She had been in the army for a while, but they kicked her out because of her unpredictable behavior. Now, she worked out at the gym, hung out at the mall, and mostly just freaked people out—always dressed in army clothes and talking about shooting guns. Conventional wisdom stated that you should just stay away from her. And that's what Artie and Billy did from that point onwards. Both of them stopped working at Media Hardware shortly afterwards.

Sylvia's neighbors often complained to Tim, the building manager, about her loud music, screaming, shouting, and aggressive behavior. She sometimes came into the hardware store and spooked customers there too. Tim did what he could to handle the situation, and most often all he could do was to call Ruth Seegrist, Sylvia's mother.

Sylvia Seegrist in 1985. Courtesy of the DA's office.

Ruth had a tough time with her daughter. Since her diagnosis ten years earlier, Sylvia's violent obsessions had increased, and she had been hospitalized a dozen times. Each time, doctors would discharge her because medication seemed to control her condition.

But she didn't like to take her meds.

Ruth tried to make things right—she came by to apologize to neighbors and clerks in the store, but she couldn't control her daughter, and besides, as Sylvia would later say in custody, "My family makes me nervous."

During the first couple of dozen Media Gothic tours, we met many people who knew Sylvia. One member of our tour remembered her from grade school and middle school, when she was a great student and good company. Another remembered her from her days in Media, when she would burst into house parties and make fake gunshot noises and demand to know where the guns were being hidden. People were fairly tolerant of eccentric behavior in town at that time, but this particular woman pushed that tolerance to the limit.

Things started to take a very serious turn when Sylvia's general threats turned into a specific one—she said she was going to bring a gun to one of Media's street festivals and open fire.

Mayor Frank Daly heard about it. The police heard about it. And at that point it became clear that Sylvia could no longer live in Media. She moved to an apartment in Crum Lynne, and it was from there that she gained notoriety for acting out on her violent fantasies.

The day before Halloween, 1985, Sylvia Seegrist bought a rifle and opened fire in the Springfield Mall, killing three and injuring another 9 people. A 24-year-old man disarmed her, thinking that it was a sick Mischief Night prank involving blank ammunition, and she was soon taken into custody.

From that day to this, she has been incarcerated, at first in Norristown state mental hospital, now in the correctional facility in Muncie. After being found guilty but insane, she is serving three life sentences for the murders.

Even now, more than thirty years later, people remember the anniversary of the fateful Springfield Mall shootings. Most people believe Sylvia, who is now in her sixties, will never earn parole. She is, however, studying psychology in the hopes that she may one day get employment in that field.

THE MOST GOTHIC PLACE IN MEDIA

120 E FRONT ST

The site where the Media Elementary School now stands has seen a lot of action in the past 200 years.

This large plot of land was just a field until the day before Valentine's Day, 1804, when a committee of seven Delaware County commissioners voted to build on the site. The county duly purchased the land and erected a large brick building over the next couple of years. Ever since then, it has been a bustling hub of daily activity—some activities more surprising than others.

THE "HOUSE OF EMPLOYMENT"

Delaware County built a large stone building here to house and provide a farm and workplace for more than 85 people. Officially, it was called the County House, or even the House of Employment, but everyone in Delco called it what it was: The poor house. Less charitable people also called it the mad house, since it also provided a home for people who were poor because, to use a technical term from the early 1800s, they were "insane and idiotic persons."

In the days before federal and state welfare systems, counties were responsible for taking care of their own poor. Because of its large Quaker population, Delaware County took this responsibility seriously, so when the famous nurse and advocate Dorothea Dix visited the site just before development in Media took off, she described it as "clean, well kept and well directed. The provisions are good and sufficient, and the food well prepared."

She also noted that a dozen of the 85 inmates were mentally ill, and though clean and well fed, they were chained up or hobbled because they were deemed incurable. There were also four cells in the basement to confine them when they got violent.

COUNTY HOUSE, MEDIA.

Delaware County Poor Farm, about 1820

The poor farm operated here for more than fifty years, until Media's real estate boom made the land so valuable, the county could sell it at a tidy profit and use that cash infusion to establish a bigger, better, and more efficient poor farm out in Middletown.

The new owner, bank president Isaac Haldeman, replaced the tired old building with a much nicer place, but his family didn't want to maintain it over the long haul, so within a few decades, it changed hands and became a famous school—and the site of one of Media's more notorious crimes.

TRAGEDY AT THE ACADEMY

If there's one thing that was more impressive than the name Swithin Chandler Shortlidge, it was his resume. By the time he came to Media in 1874, he had been running an academy for boys and young men out in West Chester for almost a decade, and had recently married. He advertised his new school far and wide to the wealthy tycoons of Philadelphia, New York, and beyond. He boasted a staff of ten teachers—all men, all graduates, one from Harvard (Shortlidge himself) and

four from Yale—and all the creature comforts that a respectable temperance town like Media could provide. For $250 a school year, young men could be fed, washed, trained, exercised, prepared for a life of academia or business, and even have a church pew reserved for them for Sunday services in the nearby Presbyterian church, where Swithin was a warden.

THE SHORTLIDGE MEDIA ACADEMY.

The Haldeman House, sold and repurposed in the 1870s as Shortlidge's Media Academy.

Yes, Professor Swithin C. Shortlidge loomed large in the education world in the last quarter of the 19th century, and his family was equally impressive. His brother Dr. Evan Shortlidge was mayor of Wilmington, his other brother Professor Joseph Shortlidge ran a similar academy in Concordville.

THE SHORTLIDGE MEDIA ACADEMY.

It was clear that Swithin Shortlidge was destined for greatness—but it wasn't clear that he was also destined for notoriety. Nothing in the first twenty years of the Shortlidge Media Academy would prepare Media for what ultimately happened. But in 1891, things changed.

Swithin Shortlidge, from the September 27, 1894 edition of the Philadelphia Times

It all started to change when Mary Jane Shortlidge died, leaving her husband to take care of five children under the age of 18. He did not cope well. He made bad investments and ran into cash flow problems. One local wag said that he

"had been a man of note, but recently has become a man of promissory note." Swithin sank into depression, and his team of teachers took control of running the school. In the process, the academy's enrollment shrank from more than 100 students to a mere 35.

Marie Shortlidge, from the September 27, 1894 edition of the Philadelphia Times

But Swithin soldiered on and after a couple of years, things seemed to turn around for the hapless professor. He began to court Marie Dixon Jones, a younger woman who was the sister of his church's pastor, and she consented to be his second wife. The two married on November 15, 1893, and after a one-day honeymoon, settled in to married life in their quarters in the Academy building.

Later, his mother in law would tell the newspapers that the newlyweds were devoted to each other. His 18-year-old son (also called Swithin) would say that he had never seen his father so happy. And the *Philadelphia Inquirer* would quote his wife as saying "Why, he wouldn't harm a hair of anyone."

And yet things fell apart for the couple only a few weeks after their wedding.

The Academy was forced to close early because a strain of the flu referred to as "the grip" had swept through the student body. Swithin sank back into depression, and started to behave erratically. He disappeared for an entire day just before Christmas and when he returned after nightfall, claimed to have taken a train into Philly and wandered around Wanamaker's department store. His family didn't believe him. They called for his brother the Mayor of Wilmington, and after a heart-to-heart, it came to light that Swithin had attempted suicide by jumping from a public building, but that a witness had prevented him. What he didn't tell his brother was that he had purchased a gun, which he intended to use to finish the job.

Then Swithin also fell sick with the grip. He retired sick to bed for all of Christmas week. On New Year's Eve, a Sunday, he got up at 10 in the morning, pulled on a pair of pants and dragged a coat over his nightgown, then stormed out of the house. His mother-in-law and son watched as Marie Shortlidge pulled a coat over her nightclothes and followed her husband out—then they kept watching as the couple walked arm in arm down Edgmont Street, greeting each churchgoer they passed, before finally turning onto Jefferson Street and out of sight.

The next thing that happened was gunfire. Repeated gunfire. Shot after shot broke through the air, and strolling churchgoers ran in the direction of fire—to Jefferson St. There they found two people lying in the gutter. One was dead in a pool of blood, and the other was sprawled over her, shouting her name.

Swithin Shortlidge, the prominent 56-year-old professor and respected parent of the parish, had shot and killed his bride and he didn't even seem to realize what he'd done.

Shortlidge was immediately taken into custody, put in restraints, and locked up. He raved all night in his cell. Four days later, as his wife was buried in her still new bridal gown, Swithin's brothers had him committed to the state asylum in Norristown. He stayed incarcerated there until the trial.

In court, Swithin was a shadow of his former self. Nobody seemed surprised when his defense team took an insanity plea. At the trial, it came out that he had attempted suicide and exhibited signs of paranoia during his incarceration—he believed the ceiling of his cell was a curtain with people hiding behind it, and was afraid they would poison him. When he was declared guilty but insane, he was delivered to the mental health system instead of jail.

But here is where things took a strange turn. A few years later, he was declared healthy, and released. At this point, he was in his early sixties, and he lived out the next three decades as a retired man. He did not return to Media, but was cared for by a succession of family members—for many years, he lived in Wallingford. There, he read, translated manuscripts from Greek and Latin, and wrote. A lot. Many of his dispatches to

his Harvard class's alumni paper survive (you can read them at archive.org), and they all read like letters from a patriarch proud of his children and grandchildren.

Swithin Chandler Shortlidge in 1902. Courtesy of the Media Historical Archive's Appleton collection.

Although he was not a big wheel in Media society anymore, emeritus Professor Shortlidge still cast a shadow over the place. His academy had survived under the management of the teachers he had hired decades before, and on such special occasions as alumni reunions, Professor Shortlidge would show up, looking like the stern but benevolent old Victorian school teacher he had been.

Eventually, he moved to Cornwall-on-Hudson in New York state, where his son was the headmaster of the local high school. It was there in August 1931 that he died, a few months after his 91st birthday. His obituary in the August 21st edition of Wilmington's daily newspaper mentioned his connection to the former mayor of that city and to the Media Academy that once bore his name. The article made a point to highlight his recent Greek translations. It mentioned his four surviving sons and daughter.

As for his marital status, the article simply states "He was married twice, his first wife being Mary Jane Johnson and his second, Marie Jones, neither of whom is living."

CRAZED BY GRIP HE SLEW HIS BRIDE

Professor Swithin C. Shortlidge Enacts a Terrible Tragedy Near His Media Academy.

Blew Out His Wife's Brains Six Weeks After Marriage.

He Fled From Home in His Night Clothes and She Followed.

Locked in a Cell, the Professor Tells of an Attempt to Leap From the City Hall Roof and Calls for the Woman He Killed.

Delaware county's little capital, the temperance town of Media, was yesterday the scene of a terrible tragedy, in

Headlines from the Philadelphia Inquirer's front-page report of the Shortlidge shooting, dated New Year's Day, 1894.

ACKNOWLEDGMENTS

The Media Gothic Walking Tour and this book began with inspiration from many sources, but two figures stand out in particular. Henry Graham Ashmead is our spirit animal. His fastidiously researched 1884 volume *History of Delaware County* has provided us with a treasure house of anecdote and historical detail—and several illustrations. Our other great inspiration is Stephen Horne Appleton, whose photographic studio operated out of his home at 341 W. State Street from 1888 to 1906. He produced and indexed thousands of pictures, from family and fraternal groups to crime scene shots, from businesses and homes to postmortem portraits. We came across Appleton's work online only a couple of years ago, after Adam Levine of the Media Historic Archives Commission scanned them over the course of several years and spearheaded the project of putting them up at www.mediahistoricarchives.org. We strongly suggest you visit the archive online to see more historic pictures like the ones they let us reproduce in this book. Thanks also to the staff and board of the Media-Upper Providence Free Library, whose building houses the archive and supports its work.

The Walking Tour on which this book is based kicked off with energetic support from the Media Business Authority, particularly Zubair Khan, and we are extremely grateful for his enabling us to run the first of our tours during Media's midweek summer tradition of Dining Under the Stars. Thanks also for early practical help and support go to Blair Digital Media and Helen Struckmann of Serenity Wellness.

Research assistance has come from many sources, but particular thanks are owed to Adam Levine, Stephanie Gaboriault and Walt Cressler of the Media Historic Archives Commission for some excellent stories, and for their permission to reproduce some beautiful historic photography in this book. Thanks also to David Sibley of On Video, Joyce Walker of Kenny's Flower Shoppe, Heather and Drew Arata of Earth & State, Tim Swierczek of Sligo's Irish Pub, and to Arthur Wilson and Gary Gustin, all of whom provided us with some great leads. Our hats are off to you.

PICTURE CREDITS

Ordinance

TO PREVENT

MEN and BOYS

FROM ASSEMBLING IN GROUPS AT

Street Corners and Other Places.

WHEREAS, It has been reported to Council, that Men, Boys and other persons, assemble in groups at the corners of and other public places, in the streets

OF MEDIA,

to the extent of three and more, and there remain at inconvenient times and seasons, to the common nuisance of pedestrians and families, traveling along the same on business, and to places of public worship.

Therefore, Be it enacted and ordained by the Burgess and Town Council of the Borough of Media, and it is hereby enacted by the authority of the same, that the High Constable and the Assistant Constables, of the said Borough, are hereby authorized, empowered and requested, to disperse all such assemblages of persons wherever found, in the limits of said Borough, FIRST by giving them notice to separate and disappear, and upon their refusing so to do, for the space of **Five Minutes** after such notice, then to arrest all such disobedient and refractory persons, and to call on private citizens to assist in such arrest if necessary and to take such offenders before the Burgess, or a Justice of Peace, whereupon the oath of said High Constable, or Assistant, or other proof, that said persons had refused to comply with said notice; the said Burgess, or Justice shall commit such persons to the **Jail of the County,** for a period of **TWENTY-FOUR HOURS,** without bail or mainprize; for which the Constable shall be entitled to receive the sum of twenty-five cents for each arrest, the Justice of the Peace, the sum of twenty-five cents for each committal, and the Keeper of the Prison, the sum of fifty cents for each person so admitted into the Jail, to be paid by the Council, upon bills presented at a regular meeting thereof, by each of said officers, with the names of the persons so arrested, committed and received, with an affidavit of the correctness of their and each of their said bills.

Enacted this Second day of November, A. D., 1870.

C. R. WILLIAMSON, President.

Attest, A. P. OTTEY, Clerk.

AMERICAN STEAM PRINT, MEDIA, PA.

CPSIA information can be obtained
at www.ICGtesting.com
Printed in the USA
BVHW060031161121
621687BV00011B/382